Experiments
With
Solids, Liquids, and Gases

CHRISTINE TAYLOR-BUTLER

Children's Press®
An Imprint of Scholastic Inc.
New York   Toronto   London   Auckland   Sydney
Mexico City   New Delhi   Hong Kong
Danbury, Connecticut

Content Consultant
Suzanne E. Willis, PhD
Professor and Assistant Chair, Department of Physics
Northern Illinois University
DeKalb, Illinois

Library of Congress Cataloging-in-Publication Data

Taylor-Butler, Christine.
  Experiments with solids, liquids, and gases/Christine Taylor-Butler.
      p. cm.—(A true book)
  Includes bibliographical references and index.
  ISBN-13: 978-0-531-26349-5 (lib. bdg.)   ISBN-13: 978-0-531-26649-6 (pbk.)
  ISBN-10: 0-531-26349-5 (lib. bdg.)   ISBN-10: 0-531-26649-4 (pbk.)
  1. Matter—Properties—Experiments—Juvenile literature. I. Title.
  QC173.36.T39 2012
  530.4078—dc22   2011010398

All rights reserved. Published in 2012 by Children's Press, an imprint of Scholastic Inc.
Printed in China 62
SCHOLASTIC, CHILDREN'S PRESS, A TRUE BOOK, and associated logos are trademarks and/or registered trademarks of Scholastic Inc.

2 3 4 5 6 7 8 9 10 R 21 20 19 18 17 16 15 14 13

Find the Truth!

Everything you are about to read is true *except* for one of the sentences on this page.

Which one is **TRUE**?

T or F   Some reptiles can walk on water.

T or F   Heavy cream is made only of liquid.

Find the answers in this book.

3

Contents

THE **BIG** TRUTH!

The Three Phases of H_2O

Hot air balloons use
helium gas to fly.

You can try this experiment (p. 25) to discover the difference between salt water and freshwater.

About two-thirds of Earth's water is frozen.

Molecules are
two or more
atoms combined.

CHAPTER 1

The States That Matter

The world is filled with **matter**. The air you breathe. The water you drink. The food you eat. Matter can exist in different forms, but these forms all have something in common. They are made of **molecules**. Think of molecules as building blocks. The electrical forces inside molecules help them to attach to each other and form a **bond**.

There are more molecules in your body than there are stars in the sky.

The Properties of Matter

The molecules in a **solid** are held together by a strong bond. A solid holds its shape. Its volume does not change.

Liquid molecules can slide around. This allows a liquid to take the shape of a container. Its volume also does not change.

Gas molecules have very weak bonds. They are free to move away from each other. Gas does not have a definite shape or volume.

These candles are in three different states: solid, liquid, and releasing gases.

A tornado is one of the most dangerous kinds of storms on Earth.

Weather is caused by water as it changes from solid to liquid to gas and back again.

Matter can change from one state to another. But something has to happen for it to change. It can only be changed when something breaks the bonds. Scientists use the scientific method to conduct experiments to study the **properties** of matter. Experiments help them understand how something will behave in different environments.

NASA scientists use an airplane nicknamed the Vomit Comet to test their hypotheses about gravity.

How It Works

This is how the scientific method works. First, a scientist pulls together all the observations about something. Next, he or she thinks up a question that the observations don't explain. Then the scientist forms a **hypothesis**. This is what the scientist believes is the correct answer to the question. It must be a statement that can be tested. Next, he or she plans out an experiment to test it.

During the experiment, the scientist writes down everything that happens. Finally, the scientist looks at how the experiment turned out and draws a conclusion.

Sometimes, the conclusion is that the hypothesis is correct. Other times, it turns out that the hypothesis was not correct. Then it's time to come up with a new hypothesis and design another experiment.

Scientists use experiments with matter to discover Earth's age.

Tennis balls
look solid, but
they contain air
pockets inside.

CHAPTER 2

A Solid State

Are all solids the same? A tennis ball is solid but changes shape when you squeeze it. A golf ball does not. When matter is in a solid state, the molecules are packed tightly together. A solid can't change unless force is applied to it.

Experiment #1: Bend, Compress, Break

Observe: Different solids look and feel different from each other.

Research question: Can a person bend, cut, crush, or break one solid as easily as another?

True Book hypothesis: Some solids are easier to bend, cut, crush, or break than others.

Materials:

▷ **long candle**
▷ **small rocks**
▷ **lump of charcoal**
▷ **lump of clay**
▷ **old spoon**
▷ **sheet of paper**

Gather these materials.

▷ **scissors**
▷ **hammer**

Solid Material	Bend	Cut	Crush	Break

Procedure:

1. Make a chart similar to the one shown above. Add an extra row for each solid you have.

2. Try bending each of the objects.

3. Try cutting the objects with scissors.

4. Push down on each object with your hands.

5. Gently tap the objects with the hammer.

Record your results: Which objects can be bent? Which can be cut or crushed? Which ones break? Make a note if any become a liquid or gas.

Conclusion: The solids did not change form, but their appearances changed. Different solids react differently to physical force. Some solids are harder or stronger than others. Does this match your observations? Was the True Book hypothesis correct?

Step 3

15

Experiment #2: Heated Hypothesis

Observe: Heat can melt a solid.

Research question: Does the amount of matter change when a solid melts?

True Book hypothesis: The amount of matter stays the same when a solid melts.

Materials:

Gather these materials

- **2 or 3 scoops of ice cream**
- **measuring cup**

Procedure:

1. Put the ice cream in the measuring cup. Mash it down so there is no space between the scoops.
2. Read the measuring cup. How much ice cream do you have?
3. Place the ice cream in a sunny window. Let it sit for 2 hours.

Record your results: Did the ice cream change form? How much ice cream is there now?

Conclusion: As the sun heated the ice cream, the ice cream molecules sped up. The ice cream became a liquid. Do you have less ice cream now than when you started? If so, the liquid was heated further and its molecules sped up even more. It turned into a gas, which mixed with the air and left the bowl. Does this match your observations? Was the True Book hypothesis correct?

When a candle burns, some of the wax evaporates into the air.

The Three Phases of H₂O

Water molecules are made from two atoms of hydrogen bonded to one atom of oxygen. Water can naturally exist in three different states in Earth's normal temperatures. These states are liquid, gas, and solid. Heat can change water from one state to another. Adding or subtracting heat changes the state of water and creates weather.

Gas

When water is heated, the molecules begin moving very fast. This allows them to move away from one another. Water becomes a gas called steam at 212 degrees Fahrenheit (100 degrees Celsius). The steam rises into the air. Heating the water into a gas is known as boiling.

Liquid

When water cools, the molecules slow down. They pack closer together. The molecules can slide, but they remain attracted to each other. This allows the liquid water to take the shape of any container it fills.

Solid

Water freezes when the temperature falls below 32°F (0°C). The molecules almost stop moving. Unlike other types of matter, the volume of water increases when it freezes. In other words, frozen water takes up more space than liquid water.

Without gravity, water would form into the shape of a sphere.

CHAPTER 3

How Do Liquids Behave?

Pour water into a glass. It pours in a stream. It takes the shape of the glass. What makes liquid stick together? What would happen if there were no container? Can you change water's properties?

Demonstration: The Shape of Water

Water takes the shape of its containers. Let's do a demonstration to see what shape water takes when it is placed on a flat surface.

Materials:
- ▶ **a dry penny**
- ▶ **magnifying glass**
- ▶ **shallow bowl**
- ▶ **tap water**
- ▶ **black pepper**
- ▶ **dish soap**

Procedure:

1. Place a drop of water on the penny.
2. Examine the water with your magnifying glass. What shape does it make? Is it flat or curved?
3. Fill the bowl with water.
4. Sprinkle a teaspoon of pepper into the bowl.
5. Rub dish soap on your finger and dip it into the middle of the bowl.

Step 4

Step 5

Observe: What shape did the water make on the penny? Did the pepper float on the water in the bowl? What happened to the pepper when you dipped a soapy finger into the water?

What happened? Water molecules are sticky. They attract one another. Molecules on the surface form a temporary skin. This is called surface tension. It's what makes the surface of water curve. Light objects can rest on the surface of water. The soap on your finger breaks the surface tension. It makes the water flatten out. As a result, the pepper slides to the edge of the bowl.

Walking on Water

Water striders are very small insects. Their long, thin legs are covered in tiny hairs. The hairs allow them to walk on water without breaking the surface tension. This basilisk is a much larger reptile. It has special feet that allow it to run on water for up to 14 feet (4.3 meters) before sinking. Scientists are studying these creatures. They would like to invent shoes that will allow humans to walk on water!

Experiment #1: Changing Properties

Observe: Ocean water has salt. The freshwater in rivers, lakes, and in your home does not.

Research question: Does adding matter, such as salt, change a liquid's properties?

True Book hypothesis: Salt changes the properties of water.

Materials:

- **2 water glasses**
- **measuring cup**
- **water**
- **1 raw egg in the shell**
- **salt**
- **red food coloring**

It is best to use clear glasses in this experiment.

25

Procedure:

1. Fill each glass with 1 cup (250 milliliters) of hot tap water.
2. Add red food coloring to one glass.
3. Now put the egg in the red water. What happens?
4. Stir 0.25 cup (38 ml) of salt into the second glass.
5. Slide the egg into the salt water. What happens?
6. Pour some of the red water into the salt water glass.

Step 5

Record your results: In which glass does the egg float? What happens when the freshwater is added to the salt water?

Conclusion: A salt molecule and a water molecule can fit more tightly together than two water molecules can. This means salt water has a higher **density**. An egg is denser than freshwater, so it sinks. But the egg is not as dense as salt water. This allows the egg to float. In Step 6, the less-dense freshwater (red) also floats. How does this conclusion compare to your observations? Was the True Book hypothesis correct?

Step 6

Hot air balloons rise because the heated gas inside the balloon is lighter than the air outside of it.

CHAPTER 4

Gas All Around You!

Can you see air? No, it's invisible. Cut a strip of paper. Hold it in front of you. Now blow on it. It moves. This proves air exists. It can have force and push on something, just like the wind outside can push a kite. What other observations can we make about how air behaves?

Experiment #1: There's Air in There!

Observe: A clean water or soda bottle looks empty.

Research question: Does the bottle contain very much air?

True Book hypothesis: Air can be added to an empty bottle.

Materials:

- measuring cup
- empty plastic soda bottle
- 1 empty balloon
- 1 drinking straw

Procedure:

1. Slide the balloon inside the bottle.

2. Cover the mouth of the bottle with the lip of the balloon.

3. Try to blow air into the balloon. Can you inflate it?

4. Uncover the lip of the balloon from the bottle.

5. Slide a straw into the bottle next to the balloon.

6. Try to blow air into the balloon again.

7. Try to remove the balloon. Can you?

Step 3

Record your results: What happened when you tried to blow up the balloon the first time? What happened when you added a straw?

Conclusion: When you first try to inflate the balloon, the air inside the bottle is trapped. The molecules pack tighter together. This creates pressure inside the bottle. The air pushes against the balloon. Adding the straw lets the air inside the bottle escape when you inflate the balloon. You can't remove the balloon because the air in the balloon has replaced the air in the bottle. Does this match your observations? Was the True Book hypothesis correct?

Step 6

What happens? Gas doesn't have a shape or a fixed volume. Its molecules are constantly moving. They can move closer or farther from each other. Because of this, gas is the only type of matter that can be squeezed to fit in a smaller space. It can also expand to fill a larger space.

Experiment #2: Making a Gas

Observe: Chemical reactions can change solids and liquids into different forms.

Timeline of Experiments with Solids, Liquids, and Gases

4th century B.C.E.

Aristotle discusses the states of matter.

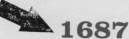

1687

Isaac Newton first describes the affect of motion on matter.

Research question: Can liquids and solids be changed into gases?

True Book hypothesis: Liquids and solids can be changed into gases.

Materials:
- measuring cup
- empty plastic soda bottle
- 2 empty balloons
- small cone or funnel
- white vinegar
- baking soda

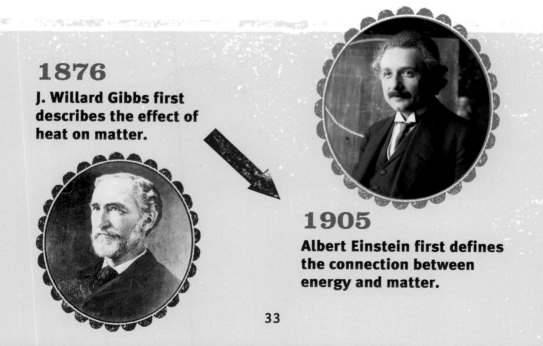

1876
J. Willard Gibbs first describes the effect of heat on matter.

1905
Albert Einstein first defines the connection between energy and matter.

Procedure:

1. Pour 0.25 cup (38 ml) of vinegar into the empty bottle.
2. Pour one tablespoon (15 ml) of baking soda into the second balloon, using a cone or small funnel.
3. Place the neck of the balloon over the mouth of the bottle. Make a tight seal.
4. Raise the balloon until it is straight up in the air.
5. Shake the baking soda into the bottle.

Step 2

Record your results: What happens to the vinegar and baking soda? What happens to the balloon?

Conclusion: Baking soda is made of sodium bicarbonate. Vinegar is an acid. When the two combine, they create a chemical reaction. Vinegar causes the baking soda to break down, creating a different substance. This is a gas called carbon dioxide. It is less dense than the air around it. The carbon dioxide rises into the balloon, inflating it. Does this match your observations? Was the True Book hypothesis correct?

Step 5

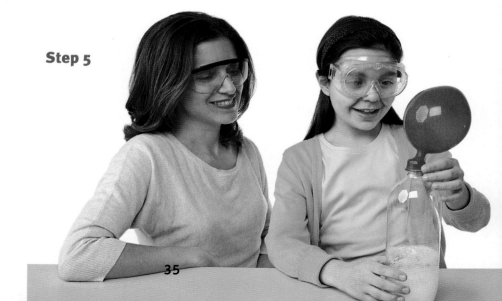

Colloids

Have you ever whipped egg whites for a recipe? How about whipping heavy cream for a dessert? How does a liquid suddenly change into a thick cream if you don't add anything to it? The answer is that egg whites and heavy cream are **colloids**. A colloid is a substance that contains more than one type of matter. One type is evenly **dispersed,** or mixed, throughout the other. Paint, milk, gelatin, cheese, and aerosols are examples of colloids.

 Whipped cream is a colloid.

Step 3

Experiment #1: Whipping Up a Colloid

Observe: Colloids can change form.

Research question: Can a liquid turn into a solid without adding anything but air?

True Book hypothesis: A liquid colloid can turn into a solid by adding air.

Materials:
- measuring cup
- 1 cold bowl
- 2 raw eggs
- fork

Procedure:

1. Crack both eggs.
2. Separate the egg whites into the measuring cup. Record their volume.

3. Put the egg whites in the cold bowl and whip them with a fork.

4. After one minute, record your observations.

5. Keep whipping the egg whites until they form stiff peaks.

6. Add the whipped egg whites to the measuring cup. Record their volume.

Record your results: Do the egg whites have more volume than when you started?

Conclusion: Whipping the egg whites forces air to mix with the liquid. Air becomes dispersed through the egg whites. As more air is trapped, the mixture's volume grows. The difference in volume is the amount of air trapped in your colloid. Does this match your observations? Was the True Book hypothesis correct?

Colloids Versus Suspensions

A suspension is not the same as a colloid. What is a suspension? If solid particles are mixed with water, the particles will stay suspended for a while. Then some of the particles will begin to settle to the bottom of the glass. Another example of a suspension is fresh cow's milk. A person can separate some of the substances dispersed in milk to make cheese. The other substances are left behind as whey. However, in a colloid, the solids will stay dispersed.

Experiment #2: Try It Again!

Research question: Can heavy cream be turned into a solid by adding air?

True Book hypothesis: Heavy cream can be turned into a solid by whipping it.

Materials:

- **measuring cup**
- **cold bowl**
- **fork**
- **1 cup (250 ml) heavy cream**

Procedure:

1. Pour 1 cup (250 ml) heavy cream into a clean, cold bowl.

2. Whip the cream with a fork.

3. Repeat steps 4 through 6 of the previous experiment. (p. 39)

Where you able to turn the liquid cream into a solid?

Record your results: Can the heavy cream be turned into a solid? How long does it take?

Conclusion: Heavy cream is butterfat dispersed in liquid milk. When you whip the cream, air gets trapped between the solid butterfat molecules and the liquid becomes a solid. Does this conclusion match with your observations? Was the True Book hypothesis correct?

Do you have more questions about solids, liquids, and gases? Try some experiments using the scientific method to find the answers! ★

Oil and vinegar form a suspension. They cannot mix like a colloid.

Smallest molecule: A molecule made up of two hydrogen atoms

Most unusual place to find a water molecule: On the moon

Hardest natural solid: A diamond

Hardest human-made solid: Carbon steel

Lightest gas on Earth: Hydrogen

Heaviest gas on Earth: Radon

Average amount of air breathed by humans each day: 3,000 gal. (11,355 l)

Average number of breaths by a human in a lifetime: 625 million

Did you find the truth?

T Some reptiles can walk on water.

F Heavy cream is made only of liquid.

Resources

Books

Boothroyd, Jennifer. *Many Kinds of Matter: A Look at Solids, Liquids, and Gases.* Minneapolis: Lerner, 2011.

Claybourne, Anna. *The Nature of Matter.* Milwaukee: Gareth Stevens, 2007.

Hurd, Will. *Changing States: Solids, Liquids, and Gases.* Chicago: Heinemann Library, 2009.

Spilsbury, Richard, and Louise Spilsbury. *What Are Solids, Liquids, and Gases? Exploring Science With Hands-on Activities.* Berkeley Heights, NJ: Enslow, 2008.

Stille, Darlene. *Solids, Liquids, and Gases.* Chanhassen, MN: Child's World, 2005.

Tocci, Salvatore. *Experiments With Water.* New York: Children's Press, 2002.

Tocci, Salvatore. *Experiments With Weather.* New York: Children's Press, 2003.

West, Krista. *States of Matter: Gases, Liquids, and Solids.* New York: Chelsea House, 2008.

Organizations and Web Sites

American Museum of Natural History—Water: H_2O = Life

www.amnh.org/exhibitions/water

Click on the "Blue Planet" link to learn more about the three phases of water.

Science Kids—Science Games for Kids: Solids, Liquids and Gases

www.sciencekids.co.nz/gamesactivities/gases.html

Learn about the states of matter in this simple interactive game.

Places to Visit

Children's Museum of Houston

1500 Binz
Houston, TX 77004
(713) 522-1138
www.cmhouston.org
FlowWorks, a hands-on exhibit about the properties of water.

Children's Museum of Indianapolis

3000 North Meridian Street
Indianapolis, IN 46208-4716
(317) 334-3322
www.childrensmuseum.org
Learn about nature's solids: rocks, minerals, and fossils.

Important Words

bond (BAHND)—an electric attraction that holds molecules together

colloids (KAH-loydz)—substances in which particles of one type of matter are dispersed throughout another type

density (DEN-si-tee)—the amount of material packed into a unit of space; a measure of how heavy or light an object is for its size

dispersed (dis-PURSD)—evenly mixed substances

gas (GAS)—a substance that will spread to fill any space that contains it

hypothesis (hy-PAH-thuh-siss)—a prediction that can be tested about how a scientific experiment or investigation will turn out

liquid (LIK-wid)—matter that can change shape but not size

matter (MAT-ur)—something that has weight and takes up space, such as a solid, liquid, or gas

molecules (MAH-luh-kyoolz)—the smallest individual units that a chemical compound can be divided into that still display all of its chemical properties

properties (PROP-ur-teez)—the special characteristics or qualities of something

solid (SAH-lid)—matter that does not easily change shape or size

Index

Page numbers in **bold** indicate illustrations

About the Author

Christine Taylor-Butler is the award-winning author of more than sixty books for children including a True Book series on American Government as well as another on Health and the Human Body. A graduate of the Massachusetts Institute of Technology (MIT), she is passionate about finding fun ways to introduce science, technology, engineering and math (STEM) concepts to children. Christine lives in Kansas City, Missouri.